Tower Power

Tales from the Tower of London

CONTENTS

Welcome ...

...to the Tower of London! It is one of the largest and most important castles in England. But who built it? And why? Use this map to guide you round – and discover the answers for yourself.

The Tower in Norman times

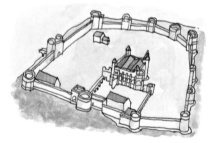

The Tower in the Middle Ages

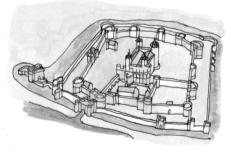

The Tower in Tudor times

Key

① *Beauchamp Tower*

② *Bloody Tower*

③ *Bowyer Tower*

④ *Chapel Royal of St Peter ad Vincula*

⑤ *Cradle Tower*

⑥ *Lion Tower Drawbridge Pit*

⑦ *Martin Tower*

⑧ *Middle Tower*

⑨ *Mint Street*

⑩ *Moat*

⑪ *New Armouries*

⑫ *Ravens' Lodgings*

⑬ *Roman Wall*

⑭ *Salt Tower*

⑮ *Scaffold Site*

⑯ *St Thomas's Tower*

⑰ *The Crown Jewels*

⑱ *Tower Green*

⑲ *Tower Hill*

⑳ *Traitors' Gate*

㉑ *White Tower*

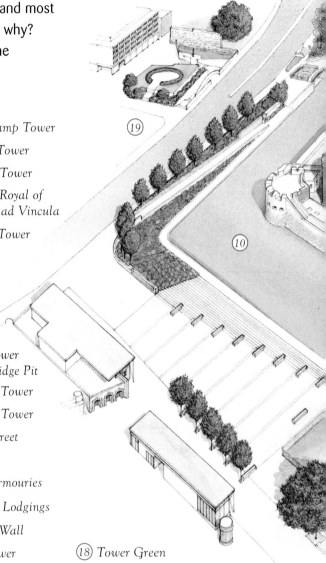

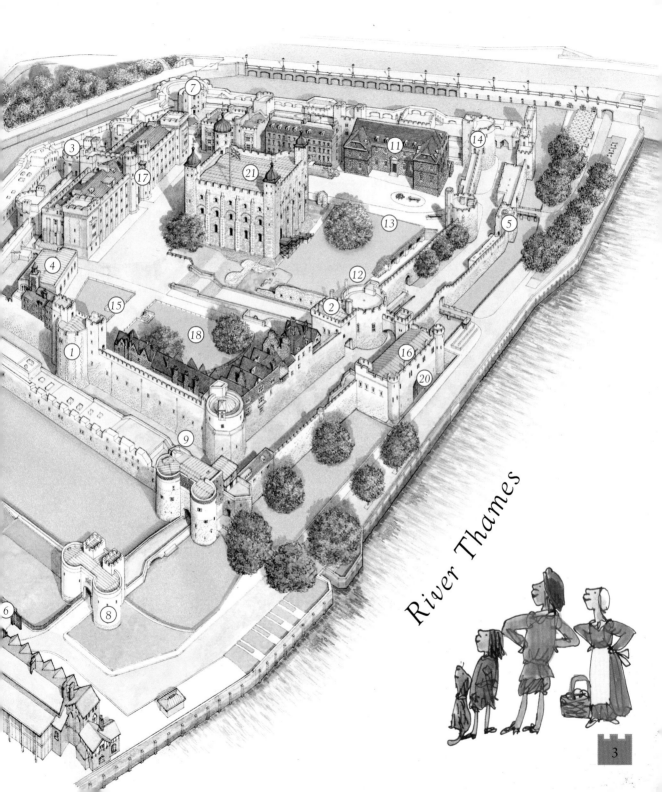

River Thames

3

The Conqueror's Tower

The oldest part of the Tower of London is the White Tower. William of Normandy built it soon after he conquered England at the Battle of Hastings in 1066.

A silver penny with the head of William the Conqueror.

The Saxons didn't like their new Norman king. So William built the Tower of London to protect himself from attack – and to show Londoners that he was boss. Houses were knocked down to make way for the castle and Saxons were forced to build it. That made him even more unpopular!

William's castle was HUGE. Most other buildings in London were wooden and only one storey high, so the Tower could be seen for miles around. No one in England had seen anything like it before. It was all a bit scary!

Saxons building a Norman castle with picks and shovels. ▶

STELLVM: AT HESTENGA CEASTRA

William's castle was whitewashed about 200 years after it was built. It's been called the White Tower ever since.

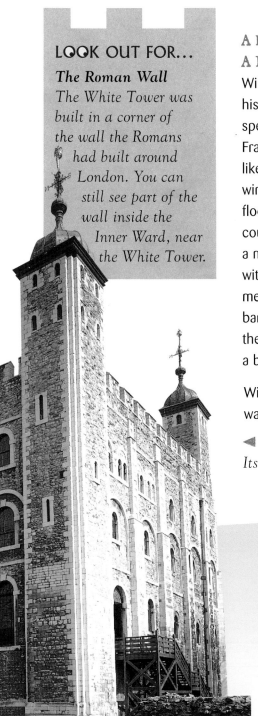

LOOK OUT FOR...

The Roman Wall

The White Tower was built in a corner of the wall the Romans had built around London. You can still see part of the wall inside the Inner Ward, near the White Tower.

A FORTRESS AND A PALACE

William used stone to build his castle. Some of it was specially brought from France. Outside it was built like a fortress with small windows and a door at first floor level so that attackers couldn't get in. Inside it was a magnificent royal palace with large rooms for meetings, trials and banquets, private rooms for the King and his family, and a beautiful chapel.

▲ *The Chapel of St John the Evangelist in the White Tower.*

William died in 1087, before the White Tower was finished. His son William Rufus completed it.

◄ *The White Tower is nearly 30 metres high. Its walls are more than 4 metres thick.*

William's castle was very comfortable. It had fireplaces to heat the rooms and garderobes (toilets). Remember, most Londoners lived in cold and filthy conditions then.

5

A Mighty Fortress

About 150 years later Henry III, and then his son Edward I, made the castle larger and stronger. When Edward died in 1307, the Tower of London was the mightiest castle in the land.

In the 1230s, Henry III quarrelled with his barons and fled to the Tower for safety. While he was there he realised that the defences weren't strong enough to keep attackers out. Help!

Henry ordered MASSIVE, new stone walls and eight giant towers. The towers opened on to walkways so that archers could keep a good look out for attackers. Henry dug a new, wide moat with dams to keep water in at low tide.

Can you spot the siege engine? ▶

▲ *Henry III*

▲ *The Tower was equipped with siege engines that could hurl huge stones 200 metres or more.*

Henry III kept an elephant at the Tower. It was probably the first time anyone had seen an elephant in England.

BIGGER AND BETTER

Edward I was a great warrior king and famous for building castles. He spent MILLIONS (in today's money) on another, outer wall that wrapped round the whole castle. This made it one of the biggest and most important castles in the country.

Edward made the main entrances much stronger with stone bridges across the moat, heavy wooden gates and murder holes (for dropping missiles or boiling water on to attackers).

This picture shows one of Edward I's great towers and his new wall in front of it. ▼

LOOK OUT FOR...

A wooden portcullis

that dropped down to stop attackers getting in. It was raised and lowered with ropes and pulleys. This one still works – so watch out!

Under Attack!

The Tower was only attacked five or six times. One of the oddest raids happened in the Middle Ages, when it was invaded by a mob of angry peasants.

In 1381, peasants were fed up with high taxes (money people had to pay to the king). Thousands marched to London looting and burning everything in their way. It was so terrifying that Richard II and his family, his nobles and Simon of Sudbury, the Archbishop of Canterbury, fled to the Tower for safety.

Some of the rebels followed and camped outside the Tower. King Richard, who was then only 14 years old, agreed to meet the leaders. As the Tower gates opened to let Richard out, the mob rushed in and headed straight for his apartments!

▲ *Can you spot the Mayor of London killing Wat Tyler and Richard speaking to the peasants?*

The soldiers on duty were so terrified at the sight of hundreds of angry peasants armed with sticks, spades and scythes, they froze to the spot!

WHAT HAPPENED NEXT?

The following day King Richard met the mob and their leader, Wat Tyler. But as Wat came forward to speak to the King, the Mayor of London killed him.

It was a very dangerous moment for Richard – the mob could have easily turned on him. But showing great courage, he persuaded the peasants to accept him as their leader and to go home. Later, the other leaders of the mob were arrested and hanged.

▲ *The Archbishop of Canterbury's head was stuck on a spike and displayed on London Bridge.*

The peasants stole weapons and jewels. They pulled nobles' beards, lounged about on the King's bed and were very cheeky to the King's mother.

The King's mother was rescued but some nobles and the Archbishop of Canterbury were beheaded on Tower Hill.

Hello. Queenie.

Dirty Deeds

Terrible things took place in the Tower. The story of two young princes who 'disappeared' while staying at the Tower is a horrible crime that has never been solved.

When Edward IV died in 1483 his son, 12-year-old Prince Edward, succeeded him. Edward was too young to rule so his uncle Richard, Duke of Gloucester stood in for him. Prince Edward and his younger brother, 9-year-old Prince Richard, were moved to the Tower. Shortly afterwards, the Duke of Gloucester had himself crowned Richard III.

▲ *Most people think Richard III had the two princes murdered. But no one can prove it!*

THE PRINCES DISAPPEAR

The princes were last seen alive in the Tower during the summer of 1483. Almost 200 years later, the skeletons of two boys aged about 10 and 12 were discovered near a staircase in the White Tower. Could these have been the princes?

◀ *This painting shows the two princes being murdered in their sleep. But no one really knows what happened to them.*

LOOK OUT FOR...
*A **secret hiding place** where the bones of two young boys were discovered. You can see it as you go up the stairs to the White Tower. The bones now rest in Westminster Abbey.*

Christopher Wright

Iohn Wright

Robert Winter

Thomas Percy

Guido Fawkes

Robert Catesby

Thomas Winter

Bates

TORTURE

Although the Tower is famous for torture and punishment, as far as we know only 48 people were actually tortured there. One of them was Guy Fawkes who was arrested and taken to the Tower after trying to blow up the Houses of Parliament in 1605. Guy refused to answer any questions. To make him confess, he was tortured by stretching his body on a rack.

Later he was executed.

▲ *Can you spot Guy (Guido) Fawkes?*

Cheers!

Prince Llewelyn of Wales was killed in battle in 1282. Edward I had his head cut off, crowned with ivy and stuck on a spike at the Tower.

In 1478 George, Duke of Clarence was imprisoned for plotting against Richard III. Legend says he was executed by drowning in a barrel of wine in the Bowyer Tower.

A Royal Palace

In the Middle Ages, kings built themselves splendid apartments at the Tower. But none of them stayed there for very long, because they had lots of castles and palaces in other parts of the country.

Anne Boleyn

Henry VIII was the last king to build royal apartments at the Tower. He decided that the Tower wasn't smart enough for his second wife, Anne Boleyn. He had buildings repaired and redecorated so that she could stay there before her coronation in 1533. Three years later, she stayed in the same rooms as a prisoner and was executed on Tower Green.

▲ *The coronation procession of Charles II. Can you spot him on his white horse?*

When Charles II became king in 1660, the royal apartments had become very shabby. So he stayed at Westminster Palace before his coronation.

Coronation day at last!

Your breakfast sir

Your hat and coat sir

Your best wig sir

CORONATION DAY

It was the custom for kings and queens to stay at the Tower on the night before their coronation. The next day they started out for Westminster Abbey where they were crowned. Today, the procession starts from Buckingham Palace.

At the crack of dawn Charles set off in a boat for the Tower so that his coronation procession could start from there.

Faster! faster!

LOOK OUT FOR...
St Thomas's Tower

Edward I built new rooms for himself overlooking the river. Underneath was a watergate (now called Traitors' Gate) so that he could enter the castle in his royal barge.

13

Sent to the Tower

The Tower of London was not built to be a prison and there are no dungeons. But it was a strong building – so prisoners were kept there from the beginning.

In the Middle Ages, many prisoners were important men captured in war and held in exchange for LARGE RANSOMS (money). They were usually kept in nice rooms with furniture and fires – they had to be well looked after until the ransom was paid.

The Duke of Orleans was captured in battle. He was kept prisoner in the White Tower. Can you spot the messenger arriving with the ransom? ▶

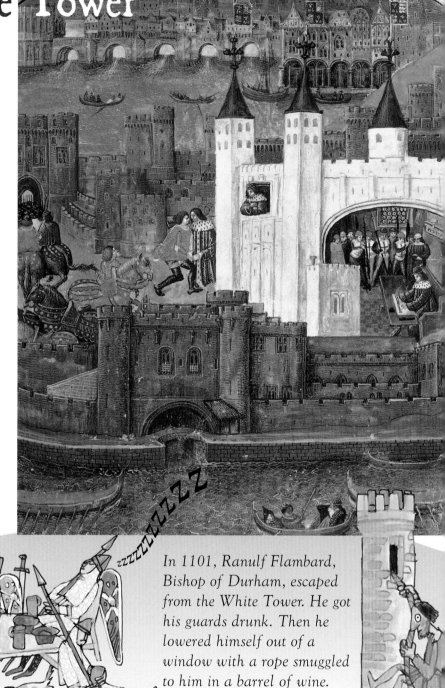

In 1101, Ranulf Flambard, Bishop of Durham, escaped from the White Tower. He got his guards drunk. Then he lowered himself out of a window with a rope smuggled to him in a barrel of wine.

TERRIBLE TIMES

In Tudor times, many more prisoners were sent to the Tower. Some had disagreed with the king or queen about religion. Others were imprisoned because they might plot to seize the throne.

Prisoner facts in Henry VIII's reign

✠ 112 people were kept prisoner in the Tower
✠ 101 were men
✠ 69 were executed
✠ 22 were lords or important churchmen
✠ 11 were women
✠ 11 were Henry's relations
✠ 7 were prisoners of war
✠ 4 were tortured

TRAITORS' GATE

Until about 200 years ago most people arrived at the Tower by river. It was quicker than travelling through narrow streets by horse or carriage. In Tudor times, so many prisoners entered by this watergate, it became known as Traitors' Gate.

LOOK OUT FOR...
Prisoners' carvings

Some prisoners carved their names, signs or messages into the stone walls of their cells. Look for them in the Salt Tower or the Beauchamp Tower.

◀ *Traitors' Gate*

More oranges Father?

In 1599, Father John Gerard escaped from the Cradle Tower. He sent his escape plan to his friends written in invisible ink made with orange juice!

15

Arms and Armour

The Tower was a royal fortress so it supplied and stored all the weapons, armour and equipment for kings' armies and warships.

In the Middle Ages, the Tower was defended with siege engines and soldiers armed with longbows and crossbows. By the time Henry VIII became king in 1509, the Tower was defended with cannon.

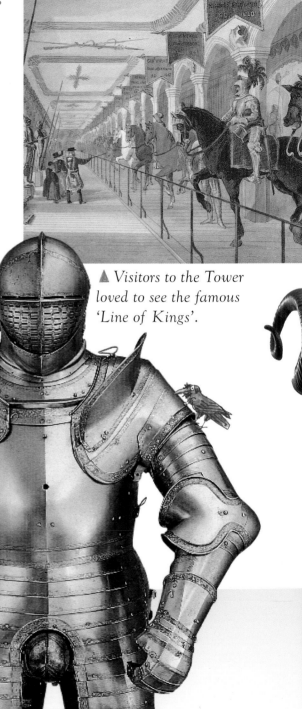

▲ *Visitors to the Tower loved to see the famous 'Line of Kings'.*

Fighting facts

In 1327, these weapons were stored in the Tower:

- 10,070 crossbow bolts and 94 crossbows
- 101 iron helmets and 1 gold helmet with leather padding
- 74 shields
- 51 pairs of plate-armour gloves
- 36 bundles of arrows
- 25 lances tipped with steel
- 8 coats of chain mail
- 2 siege engines

This armour, made for Henry in 1540, was for fighting on foot. ▶

JUST IN CASE

When Henry became king in 1509, he was worried that England would be invaded. He ordered lots of new weapons, guns and gunpowder and stored them in the Tower.

ARMOUR FOR SHOW

Henry set up royal workshops in Greenwich to make the finest armour for himself and his rich nobles. He kept some of his suits of armour in the Tower which you can still see today.

Henry wore this armour at an important meeting with the French king, Francis I. ▶

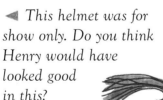

◀ *This helmet was for show only. Do you think Henry would have looked good in this?*

OUCH!

neighhhh!

Once, during a tournament, Henry fell off his horse. The horse then fell on top of him and he was badly injured.

17

Off with their Heads!

squawrkkk.

The Tower was a place of execution. Seven people met their deaths on Tower Green – four of them on the orders of Henry VIII!

The people beheaded were all accused of plotting against the king or queen (called treason). 500 years ago, most people accused of treason (traitors) were either burnt at the stake or hanged, their innards taken out and their bodies cut into four pieces. So people thought beheading was an easy death!

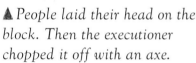

▲ *People laid their head on the block. Then the executioner chopped it off with an axe.*

A king watches as a traitor is beheaded. ▶

Anne Boleyn was beheaded with a sword. She knelt upright as the executioner snatched the sword hidden behind some straw and cut off her head with a single blow.

TOWER GREEN

This is where special prisoners were beheaded in private – away from jeering crowds on Tower Hill where most traitors were executed. Robert Devereux was executed here because he was so popular that a public execution might have caused a riot.

People executed on Tower Green

✠ 1483 Lord Hastings
✠ 1536 Anne Boleyn, Henry VIII's second wife
✠ 1541 Margaret Pole, Countess of Salisbury
✠ 1542 Catherine Howard, Henry VIII's fifth wife
✠ 1542 Viscountess Rochford, Catherine's lady-in-waiting
✠ 1554 Lady Jane Grey, the 'nine day queen'
✠ 1601 Robert Devereux, Earl of Essex

▲ Lady Jane Grey was only 16 when she was beheaded. This picture was painted much later in Victorian times. Do you think the artist felt sorry for her?

HELP!

Margaret Pole, aged 70, refused to put her head on the block. She ran screaming round the scaffold, chased by the executioner and was beheaded after several goes!

aaarrrrrgghhh!

Come back madam
OY!
Won't take a minute

LOOK OUT FOR...

The place that marks where the scaffold may have stood on Tower Green. It was a wooden platform built specially for executions.

19

The Crown Jewels

The Crown Jewels are part of the precious and religious objects used in the English coronation ceremony. They have been kept at the Tower since the Middle Ages.

Queen Elizabeth II wearing the Imperial State Crown. She holds the Sovereign's Orb and Sceptre. ▶

LOOK OUT FOR...

The Coronation Spoon

This spoon is about 800 years old. It is used to put holy oil on the king or queen during the coronation ceremony. It was sold off to a faithful servant of Charles I. When Charles II became king, the spoon was returned.

In 1649, Charles I was executed and Oliver Cromwell took control of the country. He ordered the Crown Jewels to be broken up, melted down and the precious stones sold off. When Charles II became king in 1660, he ordered a new set for his coronation. Many of them have been used at every coronation since, including that of Queen Elizabeth II in 1953.

No thanks

Legend says the Koh-i-Noor diamond brings bad luck to men but good luck to women.

Today, it is set in Queen Elizabeth, The Queen Mother's Crown.

Crown Jewels facts

✠ St Edward's Crown is the oldest crown at the Tower of London

✠ The Imperial State Crown is set with 2,868 diamonds, 17 sapphires, 11 emeralds, 5 rubies and 273 pearls

✠ The Ampulla is in the shape of an eagle. It holds holy oil which is poured through a hole in its beak

✠ The Grand Punch Bowl used for coronation banquets weighs 1/4 tonne

The Imperial State Crown

Lovely! Just what I wanted

One of the largest diamonds in the world is set in the Sovereign's Sceptre. It was discovered in South Africa about 100 years ago and given to Edward VII as a birthday present.

Stop Thief!

Today, the Crown Jewels are kept in specially protected cases. But in the 1600s, they were on show behind weak wooden bars in the Martin Tower. It was only a matter of time before someone tried to steal them!

In 1671, Colonel Thomas Blood and a woman went to the Tower to see the Crown Jewels. They were disguised as a clergyman and his wife. After several visits, Mr Edwards, the keeper in charge of the jewels, and Colonel Blood became friends. They decided that Mr Edwards's pretty daughter would make a good wife for Colonel Blood's rich nephew and arranged for them to meet.

▲ *Colonel Blood*

◀ *The orb was dented in the raid.*

In 1841, a serious fire broke out near the Jewel House. But no one could find the keys! The keepers had to hack the bars apart with an axe and pull the jewels out.

NO KEYS?

NO KEYS?

NO KEYS!

 22

▲ Can you spot the changes the cartoonist has made to the real story?

THE PLAN GOES WRONG

Colonel Blood arrived with two helpers including his 'nephew'. One man kept watch outside, while the others pretended to wait for Mr Edwards's daughter. Then Colonel Blood asked to look at the Crown Jewels. Once they were in the basement where the jewels were kept, Mr Edwards was knocked out and tied up. Colonel Blood grabbed the crown and hid it under his cloak, another thief stuffed the orb down his breeches, while the other seized the sceptre.

Then their luck ran out! Mr Edwards's soldier son suddenly appeared on leave from his regiment. The robbers panicked and dropped the jewels.

Charles II at his coronation. ▶

A HAPPY ENDING

The thieves were captured but Colonel Blood refused to speak to anyone except Charles II. The King was so impressed by his cheekiness, he rewarded Colonel Blood with money and land in Ireland. And Mr Edwards's daughter married the man who captured him!

During the Second World War, the Crown Jewels were moved to a secret hiding place for safety.

Making Money

A mint is where coins are made. There were several mints in England, but for over 500 years, the one at the Tower was the most important.

Edward I set up the Mint at the Tower in the 1270s. Most of the coins of his reign had become worn out. Others had become damaged when people tried to clip off the outer edges and sell the metal. Edward built a mint in the Tower so that he would have more control over his coins.

MAKING COINS

Coins were made by STRIKING. Small pieces of metal called blanks were placed between two engraved tools (called dies) that pressed the design on to them.

In the 1700s, coins were made by machines, so making money became much quicker. Soon the Mint became too large for the Tower and it was moved to Tower Hill.

▶ *Two men operate a machine like a giant screw for making coins.*

◀ *This silver coin is called a groat. It was one of the first types of coin to be made at the Tower.*

In 1798, James Turnbull held up everyone working at the mint and made off with 2,308 coins!

Tee-hee-hee!

LOOK OUT FOR...
Mint Street on the map on page 3. This is where old money was melted down and new coins were made. Today, an exhibition, 'Coins and Kings: The Royal Mint at the Tower', can be found in Mint Street.

▲ When this coin was made in 1489, it was the largest in England.

▲ In 1797, there were not enough silver coins to go round. So the government had to put the head of George III on Spanish dollars!

▲ This gold coin is a guinea. It was one of the last coins to be made at the Tower.

The King's Menagerie

Kings and queens were often given wild animals as presents. For over 600 years, the rulers of England kept a collection of animals at the Tower.

▼ Once, when a keeper left a door open, two tigers came face to face with a lion. The lion came off worse and died a few days later.

The animals were kept to amuse royalty and their visitors. Some liked to watch one creature fighting another, and to bet on which one would win.

We don't know much about the conditions in which the animals were kept. But until Victorian times, visitors were allowed in with the monkeys, lion cubs wandered around loose and a boy was allowed to ride a zebra!

In 1251, a polar bear was given to Henry III by the King of Norway. It was tied to a long chain so that it could catch fish in the Thames.

One leopard liked to grab and snack on visitors' hats, umbrellas and bags!

LOOK OUT FOR...

The Lion Tower Drawbridge Pit

The lions were kept in a tower built with its own moat and drawbridge. The Lion Tower was pulled down long ago but you can still see the drawbridge pit.

A TOURIST ATTRACTION

From Tudor times onward, ordinary people were allowed to visit the menagerie. This is what people could see in 1741 when the first children's guidebook was written:

- 2 lions named Marco and Phillis, with their cub Nero
- 2 lionesses called Jenny and Nanny and 3 cubs
- Will the leopard
- Jenny the panther
- 2 tigers named Will and Phillis, and their cub Dick
- 1 racoon, 2 vultures and 1 porcupine
- 1 ape and a bird called a 'warwoven'.

By 1830, there were nearly 300 animals in the menagerie and there wasn't enough room to keep them. It was decided to give most of them to the zoo in Regent's Park (today's London Zoo). Others were sold to a showman and shipped to America.

▲ *Illustrations of animals in the menagerie, from the first children's guidebook.*

You silly snake

One day Mr Cops, a keeper, was holding a chicken in one hand and a large boa constrictor in the other. Suddenly, the snake darted at the bird, missed, and knotted itself round Mr Cops instead!

27

People at the Tower

Today, the Tower is no longer a prison. Nor does it have a zoo or a mint. But it's still a fortress, a palace, an armoury, a giant safe for precious things – and a home too.

Since the very beginning, lots of people have lived and worked in the Tower. It was home to Constables (who stood in for royalty when they weren't there), chaplains, porters, gaolers, guards and soldiers. Today, about 150 people live there. They are mainly the Yeoman Warders ('Beefeaters') and their families.

▲ *The ravens are looked after by a Yeoman Warder called the Ravenmaster.*

The history of the Yeoman Warders goes back to early times when they guarded the gates and prisoners. When Henry VIII was king, the King's Yeomen carried out these duties. They wore royal livery (special uniform) that is still worn today, although it has altered slightly.

▲ *The Chief Yeoman Warder in his full state uniform.*

The Duke of Wellington was Constable of the Tower for 26 years from 1826. He tried to keep visitors out because he thought they were a nuisance and a danger to security!

We're shut!

WHO GOES THERE?

The Ceremony of the Keys is a very old ceremony that still takes place every night. The Chief Yeoman Warder marches with armed soldiers to the Middle Tower. They lock the gate and march back. At the Bloody Tower a sentry steps forward and shouts, 'Halt! Who goes there?' The Chief Yeoman Warder replies, 'The keys'. 'Whose keys?' says the sentry. 'Queen Elizabeth's keys' is the reply. Then the Chief Yeoman Warder raises his hat and says, 'God preserve Queen Elizabeth!'

LOOK OUT FOR...
The Ravens

No one knows when ravens arrived at the Tower. Legend says that Charles II ordered the ravens to be killed. But someone told him that if the birds went the Tower and the kingdom would fall. So ravens have been kept at the Tower ever since – with their wings clipped so they can't fly away!

▲ The Yeoman Warders have shown visitors round the Tower since Tudor times. Can you spot the boy pretending to execute his friend with an umbrella?

Help! I'm stuck

In Victorian times the man in charge of the arms and armour liked to try on the suits of armour himself!

What happened when ...

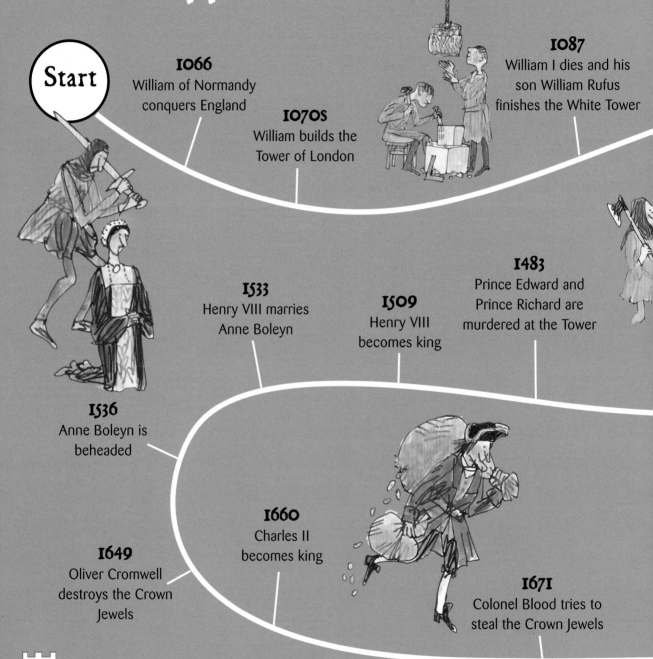

Start

1066
William of Normandy conquers England

1070S
William builds the Tower of London

1087
William I dies and his son William Rufus finishes the White Tower

1483
Prince Edward and Prince Richard are murdered at the Tower

1533
Henry VIII marries Anne Boleyn

1509
Henry VIII becomes king

1536
Anne Boleyn is beheaded

1660
Charles II becomes king

1649
Oliver Cromwell destroys the Crown Jewels

1671
Colonel Blood tries to steal the Crown Jewels

1101
Ranulf Flambard becomes the
first prisoner at the Tower

1216
Henry III becomes king.
He makes the castle larger

1272
Edward I makes the Tower of
London larger and stronger.
He sets up the mint

Hello
Queenie

1381
Peasants invade the Tower.
Richard II meets Wat Tyler

1471
Henry VI is murdered
at the Tower

1483
Richard III
becomes king

1831-2
The menagerie
is moved to
Regent's Park

1837
Victoria becomes
queen

1952
Elizabeth II
becomes queen

Historic Royal PALACES

Historic Royal Palaces is the independent charity that looks after the Tower of London, Hampton Court Palace, the Banqueting House, Kensington Palace and Kew Palace. We help everyone explore the story of how monarchs and people have shaped society, in some of the greatest palaces ever built.

We receive no funding from the Government or the Crown, so we depend on the support of our visitors, members, donors, volunteers and sponsors.

Published by Historic Royal Palaces
Hampton Court Palace
Surrey
KT8 9AU

© Historic Royal Palaces 2007

ISBN 978-1-873993-40-8

Text: Elizabeth Newbery
Design: Rachel Hamdi/Holly Mann
Editor: Clare Murphy
Illustrations: Tim Archbold
Print: City Digital Limited

Picture credits
Abbreviations: b = bottom, c = centre, l = left, r = right, t = top
The Board of Trustees of the Armouries: pages 16c, 17t, 17c, 18l, 26-7, 27; With special authorisation of the city of Bayeux/www.bridgeman.co.uk: page 4c; Photograph by Cecil Beaton/Camera Press, London: page 20t; By permission of the British Library: pages 6t (Royal 14 C VII f 9), 6-7 (Add 10294 f 81b), 8-9 (Roy 18 E I f 175), 14 (Royal MS 16 F ii f 73), 18c (Roy 20 C VII f 134v); The Trustees of the British Museum: page 4t; The Fotomas Index: pages 24-5; Crown copyright: Historic Royal Palaces: pages 2-3, 4-5, 5t, 7, 13r, 15, 28l; © Historic Royal Palaces: pages 16t, 28r, 29tr; The Peter Jackson Collection: page 23t; The Master and Fellows of Magdalene College, Cambridge: page 22tl; Courtesy of the Museum of London: pages 9t, 12-13; © The National Gallery, London: page 19t; By courtesy of the National Portrait Gallery, London: pages 10t, 11t, 12t; © HM Queen Elizabeth II 2001: pages 20l, 21, 22r; The Royal Collection © 2004 Her Majesty Queen Elizabeth II: page 23r; Courtesy of the Royal Mint: pages 24, 25; Courtesy of Sotheby's Picture Library: page 10b; Christopher Wood Gallery, London, UK/www.bridgeman.co.uk: page 29c.

www.hrp.org.uk

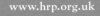